CHILDREN'S N

Seeing kids differently

PATTY BLANK

outskirtspress
DENVER, COLORADO

The opinions expressed in this manuscript are solely the opinions of the author and do not represent the opinions or thoughts of the publisher. The author has represented and warranted full ownership and/or legal right to publish all the materials in this book.

Seeing Kids Differently
Children's Numerology
All Rights Reserved.
Copyright © 2015 Patty Blank
v3.0

Cover Design © 2015 Anne Samuel. All rights reserved - used with permission.

This book may not be reproduced, transmitted, or stored in whole or in part by any means, including graphic, electronic, or mechanical without the express written consent of the publisher except in the case of brief quotations embodied in critical articles and reviews.

Outskirts Press, Inc.
http://www.outskirtspress.com

ISBN: 978-1-4787-4461-0

Outskirts Press and the "OP" logo are trademarks belonging to Outskirts Press, Inc.

PRINTED IN THE UNITED STATES OF AMERICA

Contents

We Can All "See" Differently 1
My "Sight" 2
Let's "See" 4
Lifepath 1 – My FOLLOW ME WINNER 7
Lifepath 2 – My NURTURING PEACEMAKER 12
Lifepath 3 – My HAPPY GO LUCKY JOY GIVER 17
Lifepath 4 – My DEVOTED CHILD of the EARTH 22
Lifepath 5 – My ADVENTURE SEEKER 27
Lifepath 6 – My SOFT-HEARTED LOVE CHILD 32
Lifepath 7 – My MYSTICAL VISIONARY 37
Lifepath 8 – My DYNAMIC ACHIEVER 42
Lifepath 9 – My OLD SOUL HEALER 47
Using Your "Sight" 52

We Can All "See" Differently

This book was written to aid parents, family members, educators and others involved with a child's development and growth. Yes it is a metaphysical book on children's numerology, the study of life as seen in the numbers. A kin to astrology, it is a science to understand "who we are". This life long question encompasses our minds throughout our lives. Within these pages you will discover the ancient knowledge of your child's unique gifts, thoughts, and life's goals. And even learn the negative actions they may take when things just aren't going their way. Learn their favorite colors and how to wear them. Know the common illnesses that appear when they are stressed. Read about the ways you can make them happy. And how to use the correct words of encouragement for each lifepath. With these insights you can offer them the best guidance ever!

My wish is that the knowledge of your child's lifepath will open your heart to view your authentic child from the inside out. In recognizing and understanding this incredible human being you will promote their uniqueness, develop their self-esteem, receive and realize their full potential and encourage their dreams to allow them to shine and believe wholeheartedly in themselves. Every parent, or any adult involved in the development and growth of a child, wants to provide this soul with the guidance and encouragement they require to become the adult they were designed to be.

Today our world is inhabited by too many unhappy adults that find blame in their early childhood development for their inability to succeed in life. Bad career choices, poor relationships, constant health issues, lack of encouragement in the right direction are all excuses I hear from unfulfilled people unable to make the correct decisions in life. You may be one of them. May this book open your eyes to a different way of seeing things.

> "I believe that every person is born with talent."
> -Maya Angelou

My "Sight"

Why my passion for the numbers? I grew up in the typical, low income, post World War II era, in rural Pennsylvania in a German heritage family with two older brothers. Only 15 months separated their births but they were worlds apart in their thoughts and actions. The oldest was a high achiever, always on the honor roll, first one up in the morning, rarely missed a day of school, liked riding his Schwin bike. He always dressed smart in his cords, oxford button down shirts and penny loafers decorated with dimes. He came up with the best ideas of what to do next, looked after us and always wanted to be somebody. At 16 he drove his quiet dark red English Vauxhall to work at Howard Johnson's where he dipped ice cream cones. He was mentally strong. The other brother really could care less about school, received average grades, slept in, played hooky a lot, loved hunting and fishing with my grandfather. He dressed comfortably in white T-shirts, frayed Levis and engineer boots. He was always playing sports with all his guy pals, rode his flashy stingray bike with streamers off the handle grips. He even attached bent playing cards to the spokes to make a motor sound. He did not understand the meaning of applying himself. At 16 he drove his loud, black and white '55 Chevy, with fuzzy dice hanging from the rear view mirror, dome head light painted red from the inside and a bushy fox tail waved from the antenna, to his job stocking shelves at a nearby shoe factory. He was physically strong. As the youngest and the only girl I was a good combination of both. And I was forever the brunt of the battle between these two competitive boys. Brain verses muscle was played out daily with me right in the middle.

So why were we all so different? We all grew up with the same parents, in the same house and went to the same school. In our small town most of our friends were the same as well. My parents were not the involved, preoccupied or obsessed with our strengths and/or weaknesses like my friends' parents were. They loved us each just the way we were. We had a clean house, clean clothes and were well fed. My parents were good parents.

And then there was me growing up. As a female high school senior in the seventies you either got married and started a family or you went to college after graduation. I knew my parents could not afford to send me to college. And I really wasn't directed toward any calling. I had a steady boyfriend who was a year older. A few months prior to receiving my diploma we were engaged. It happened days after he received his draft notice for the Vietnam War. My future was decided for me. Then Disney World opened the summer after my high school graduation and several of my friends who chose neither path, marriage or college, were on their way to adventure. They moved to Florida and wrote me letters about their amazing lives. Even had a huge write up in the local paper about their experiences. Me? I would play card games and go to bingo with my fiancé's mother for the next two years until he returned to marry me and start our family.

Change of plans. Oh I waited those two years, but upon his return we had both changed. I called off the wedding, started college with a business major and opened a shoe store. Over the next twelve years I quit college, endured several wonderful relationships, sold my very successful business and packed up all my stuff and moved out west. Carson City, Nevada was where I discovered numerology. A New Age friend had gifted me on my 30th birthday a complete chart of my life. It was like reading my autobiography. Written on these pages was my life; past, present and future. I wasn't a failure for not ever getting married, or not graduating from college or selling a profitable business with a strong bright future. I was living the life I was born to live. I am a FIVE! I love adventure, freedom and challenges.

Then I started gathering information on my past boyfriends, family members and close friends. For the first time in my life I understood what makes us all so different. I studied numerology for the next thirty years. It is not your parents and family, nor the environment, peer pressure or degree of education that defines you. It is all based on the very day you were born!

I have reached a point in my life that I need to stop sharing my knowledge with only my family and friends. I wrote a small novelty book on adult life path numbers eight years ago. I self-published *Birthdays, Numbers & More* but never really promoted it. I am more passionate now. I can use this metaphysical science to educate the world. Okay, so I will start with the parents of the new human beings that will be our future. I hope you enjoy what I "see".

> "Being different is one of the most beautiful things on earth."
> -Author Unknown

Let's "See"

Numerology is the easiest way to really "SEE" your children. Just understanding how they feel, think and act will help you guide and encourage them to accept themselves and increase their self-image. To calculate a Lifepath number simply add together all the numbers involved in their date of birth. Continue to add the double digits until a single digit is achieved. Example: 3-11-2007 3+1+1+2+0+0+7=14 1+4=5 In this case the child is a Lifepath 5. This is a child's birth force. Its expression is the backbone of their existence. This number describes general characteristics, trends, talents and tendencies of this new spirit so you understand them a little better. With my knowledge of numerology I have produced individual descriptions designed for children. Following each Lifepath chapter I have included a page for you to record the names (and birth dates) of all the children you know. Once you have several names connected to a child's path you will be able to understand the vibration of this group's path. This number is like a fingerprint. It is derived from the numbers of a child's day of birth and no one can change those numbers. Once you realize this you will accept every child for who they are and realize they can not be changed. You cannot change your fingerprint and you cannot change your child, or anyone else's for that matter.

Since the turn of the millennium every birth year starts with a two, the number of peace. Our birth years prior to 2000 all start with one, the number of independence. We are raising the next generation of balanced, peace loving human beings. How rewarding is that?

I need to add a short story here. In the 30 years I have been studying the numbers I have only once heard someone claim I was completely wrong with my description of them. After further investigation her mother confessed that after 18 hours of relentless, hard labor she rebelled when the nurse stated the time of birth was 12:01AM. She insisted her daughter's birthday be recorded as the 10th, not the exact day of the 11th, but rather her day of pain instead. Oh what a difference a minute made. I recalculated her Lifepath number using her actual day of birth and my friend was able to recognize herself now. I have always wondered if her determination to have a 7 path instead of a 6 path was the force behind that hard labor. Wayne Dyer says we have a day of birth and a day of death and nothing can change that. Not even a mother's request when it comes to numerology?

To better understand your little one's universal force I have just one more comparison. There are really only eight Lifepaths demonstrated by the nine individual expressions. The Lifepath NINE represents the completion or integration of all the previous eight lessons. There are some very distinct differences between the odd and the even expressions. You may want to call them opposites or opposing forces.

Odd (1,3,5,7)	Even (2,4,6,8)
Interested in what it "means".	Interested in what it "is".
Loves to have fun.	Loves to work.
Independent ambitions.	Group ambitions.
Thinks of the future in wonder.	Thinks of the past for facts.
Learns by experiencing.	Learns through education.
Where am I going?	Where have I been?
Knows a little about a lot.	Knows a lot about a little.
Creative.	Informative.
Explores the new.	Investigates the old.
Likes individual sports.	Likes team sports.

NINES are able to accept and understand all the Lifepaths. They would read down these lists by putting the word "and" between the opposing forces. The OLD SOUL HEALER really is here to teach you.

In this workbook the Lifepath number is the only calculation I will use to uncover the strongest vibration that appears in a child's chart. However you may use the single day of birth for a bit more insight. Using the example above the 11th birth day would become a 2. Reading this Lifepath number will add to your knowledge of the child. The Day of Birth number is the second strongest number that can not be changed. Later you may want to research other numbers found in their numerology make up. These numbers are calculated thorough the

◄ **SEEING KIDS DIFFERENTLY**

letters in their names and will enlighten you to their life's destiny and their soul urge, among so many other traits it is difficult to name them all here.

Almost all my friends have dogs here in the Rocky Mountains. And one day on our dog walk I realized the dogs not only looked different but they were bred to do different jobs. The spaniel took a beeline to the lake for a long swim, the lab sniffed every tree along the way until the newly aroused geese grabbed his attention, the Golden was eager to gift us with a dirty, muddy stick that would be returned many times on the walk and my Aussie was confused about which group to herd; the dogs or us, the owners. All breeds have their purpose in life. They are professionally bred to bring out the traits, talents and uniqueness of the breed. The more accomplished breeders produce show stoppers and earn the right to sell the pups for outrage amounts because they have mastered the breed prior to birth. No one can train these traits out of a breed. Believe me I would give anything if my Bleu wouldn't scare the bejesus out of every skateboarder that zoomed through my parking lot. These dogs are purebreds. Are you getting my drift? Every perfect human spirit that arrives daily on this planet is a purebred. They arrive with one of the nine paths to serve. It can not be eliminated from their DNA. They know their reason for this lifetime prior to conception. This reason is why they are now YOUR little bundle of joy. You were picked to show them the way to fulfill their dreams. Being a parent is powerful. This book will direct that power so you may raise a happy child that is encouraged to follow those dreams with confidence and joy.

> "We're all looking for the highest,
> fullest expression of ourselves as a human being."
> - Oprah Winfrey

Lifepath 1 – My FOLLOW ME WINNER

First of all, this perfect little being will use mental energy to survive in this world. He will think everything out in his head before acting. He thinks for the benefit of himself with each decision. This is a positive attribute. Look at the title, Follow Me Winner. We all aim to be one. The mind is where we get our strength. You will need to reinforce him that using his is a good thing. Encourage this with questions of thought, like "What do you think of….?"

Second, this child works with a strong male energy. Probably the most domineering male vibrations out of all nine paths. If your precious little bundle of joy is the cutest little girl ever, consider yourself lucky. You have a lot to look forward to as she takes over the world to be elected the President of the United States some day. If a child is born with an opposite energy of their gender it only shows us that their soul has evolved to the point that gender no longer is important. Just look at our world today, males and females are best friends from kindergarden, participate in the same sports together throughout their school years, co-ed dorms in college, they seek and are accepted in the same careers. We even see more fathers staying home to raise the little ones so strong ladies may become the bread winners. So please accept my use of the pronoun "he" when describing your ONE little girl. And take away all the stereotyped imagines you learned as a child. Male and female energy types are just a way to describe opposite vibrations in this evolving world of ours.

Now this one may surprise you. ONE's are introverts. You would think a male energy leader would have a lot to say. An introvert is one who is concerned primarily with his own thoughts and feelings. As a youngster he may be the "talker", running up to others, yapping away all about himself with no time to hear what they may think. Soon to realize he finds strength in keeping his thoughts and ideas to himself. Better to lead the masses if they haven't got a clue. If you are an extrovert parent you may find a pebble in your shoe with this facet of your ONE.

◂ SEEING KIDS DIFFERENTLY

One of the first things you will notice about this tiny newborn is how alert he is from day one. This little being is eager to show the world he knows exactly where he is going. He is determined from his very first breath to be the first. He will turn over and crawl early and take his first steps before he turns one. Expect him to potty train himself and learn to talk earlier than others his age. His first words will most likely be either "I", "me" or "mine" followed by "I know", "I will" and "I can". Independence is his motivation. If during his first six years of life he is challenged by a domineering parent or older sibling he will become forceful with his show of independence with statements like "We will do it my way." Or, "I'm always first". He may change the rules of the game in mid play just so he WINS. At pre-school if another toddler competes for leadership this bold number ONE will make it known that he is always right and will precede to show the rest of the class how it is done correctly. Heaven help the teacher if there are several ONE toddlers in the class.

Even at a young age ONEs like to dress to gain respect. A ONE will tuck in his shirt, match his colors, tie his shoes, parts his hair and dislikes wrinkled clothes. If your ONE is a little girl she will enjoy dresses with matching shoes, likes the newest trends and fads, will want her hair cut and styled at a young age and will even like to look good in PJs. Their favorite colors are orange, yellow, red, shocking pink and gold. They like to stand out in a crowd.

As a parent or a person of authority in his life you will take great pleasure in contributing to his independence from day one. Be willing to follow his lead. Ask him to show you how to throw a ball or ride a bike. Offer him the lead on the hiking trail. Allowing him to be first will put him in a comfort zone. Challenge him with questions that will display his abilities to consider all solutions. Actually encourage him to show his strength and leadership roles. Be proud of his ability to teach others, even at a very young age. Help him to understand and trust in his talents and traits. If you do, he may never need to prove anything to anyone. Ambitious, strong-willed, determined and well organized, the number ONE's aim is to express himself and make himself happy. Understanding fully who he is makes him truly independent, with a mind of his own.

ONEs enjoy sports and athletics, be it solo events like tennis, wrestling, swimming and skiing or team events where they excess as the home run hitter, goalie, star quarterback or team captain. ONEs mental capacity and great concentration may be void of the physical side. In which case this ONE will be the puzzle solver, chess or checker champ and captain of the debate team. Acknowledge his desire to win along with control of self in any situation for the perfect strategy. He takes pride in his abilities and the spirit to perform at the highest level. Watch out for the sore loser in him. Don't allow him to take it personally.

LIFEPATH 1 – MY FOLLOW ME WINNER

Later he may have to battle for authority with a teacher or be confused by an adult in a leadership role who sees things differently than he does. At this point he continues to justify his ability as a born leader and will strongly defend himself if only in his own mind. Pay close attention to this child during his teenage years. This is the time he may struggle with his independent role. Make an effort to ask him questions about his friends and teachers. Don't allow his quiet thoughts to get the best of your parent/child relationship. Watch your words when discussing with him, or in front of him to others, his strengths or weaknesses. You may be making comments in jest, but at this turbulent age he may introvert deeper and logically you will become one of "them" while making his world smaller. If he feels that he hasn't proven his independence prior to graduating from high school his mission in life is to prove it to the world.

Every path has its challenges and may display negativity at times. A ONE may be impatient, domineering, demanding and have a bossy manner. If he is too interested in self and his own plans he may appear selfish. Insensitive to the thoughts of others, he may often rebel the advice of others.

Other characteristics:

- Impatient of rules and regulations.
- Dislikes space cadets. If he is alert, everyone should be.
- Has a very good memory. Learns by the rote system.
- Not emotional. No kisses and hugs. May weaken him.
- A trail blazer. And a strong desire to succeed.
- Actions come from the mind not the heart.
- Not too interested in "things".
- Selective of his friends, likes them to be smart like him.
- There is always a way. Achieves his goals and then some.
- Enjoys being in the light of day. Better to see and be seen.

Health issues have their place in all vibrations. ONEs are normally in good general health and live long happy lives. As a child, bed-wetting and coughs are common. As a mentally independent, strong leader any dis-ease or opposition will come in the face of anxiety, stress, worrying, nervous disorders and uninvoked fears.

The best advise I can offer to the parent of a ONE is to show your child how to use his strengths for the good of all. The answer here lies in the vibrations of the number on either

SEEING KIDS DIFFERENTLY

side. After ONE comes TWO, the peacemaker. ONEs need to realize there is another side, another opinion besides their own, another way to find an answer. A ONE needs to learn to compromise and cooperate without losing his identity. He can stay in the driver's seat, he just needs to realize he has passengers. And since the universe is a circle, NINE would be the vibration on the other side. A ONE needs to develop compassion. Teach him to work on manifesting patience and balance. With these trades, the ONE can stop fighting to be the leader, he just "will" be the leader. He will become generous with emotions and have learned to pass on his spirit. A divine ONE will encourage others with statements like "Go for it", "Never say never", "You can do it", and "Nothing is impossible". A true ONE will have learned to be diplomatic and to restrain his forcefulness.

This being the first of the numerological commandments is, in my opinion, the most important. ONE is so basic. If you see your child wake up every morning with the desire to do the best that he can, with the right attitude and also take time to help others in his path you know he chose the right parent. If he can master this, the rest is a piece of cake.

Whatever becomes of your FOLLOW ME WINNER my wish is that you were able to recognize his individuality, boost his self-worth and accept his uniqueness.

LIFEPATH 1 — MY FOLLOW ME WINNER

These ONEs are our future entrepreneurs, Navy admirals, sports editors, computer softwear developers, jet pilots, architects, broadway producers, war monument designers, NFL promotors, trial lawyers, psychiatrists and space engineers.

_____
_____
_____
_____
_____
_____
_____

> "Before you are a leader, success is all about growing yourself.
> When you become a leader, success is all about growing others."
>
> - Jack Welsh

Lifepath 2 – My NURTURING PEACEMAKER

Your adoring little child will make all decisions emotionally, working from the heart. The most sensitive, soft-hearted, forgiving little soul to walk the earth. TWOs extrude LOVE in everything they do. Your little sweetie pie will take everything to heart. Depending on your path, whether it be an odd or even, you may be thinking "oh no" or "thank goodness". The word sensitive used to describe a child can be either threatening or inviting. Either way I hope to comfort you with my knowledge of your little TWO.

As a gentle, amiable and patient little human soul she has to be working with a highly concentrated female energy. The emotional female TWO is just as powerful as the mental male ONE. Female and male vibrations are opposing after all. One does not have power over the other. To understand both will allow you to experience them on the same level. So there is no need to fret if your little flower child is a boy. Know that he will be persuasive rather than forceful and will use influence and finesse to help others reach their goals.

TWOs are extroverts. Her first interest is to enjoy others and will always place them before herself. Harmony for this little diplomat is to unite opposing minds. A difficult feat for one who would only think of self. But this miniature peacemaker with her powers of observation and ability to understand both sides will get the job done.

From day one you will witness the peace in her eyes, the comfort in her snuggle. The TWO is an angel child, eager to please even at a young age. She is easy to toilet train, readily gives up the bottle simply because you want her to do so. She needs little discipline and rarely demands either parent's attention. The TWO is truly a blessing from birth. This may be the reason why parents seldom encourage or compliment the TWO child. They just do not feel there is a need to do so. Since TWOs respect their parents, these actions grant them an even stronger desire to obtain quiet beauty. Should she be the oldest child she will step up as

LIFEPATH 2 – MY NURTURING PEACEMAKER

mommy's little helper, babying and nurturing the younger ones. If she has older siblings with an odd path numbers they may criticize, chastise and ridicule the young TWO. She may be viewed as a weakling, a child without direction. This sweet little soul is so full of love and understanding she may never understand the teasing for she knows the ability to love and nurture others is the true key to happiness.

Comfort is the main concern when it comes to what to wear. She won't care if other kids in school are wearing fashionable, name brand clothing, it is all about the loose and soft fit. TWOs like to be free and to move. It will be challenging at time to get her out of jammys. Elastic waistbands are preferred over zip and button. You want to buy clothes that are well made with natural fibers. She will wear them out before you can hand them down. Pastels, taupes and ivories are pleasing colors, easy on the eye. But orange is a great color to help them stand out every once and awhile. Flat, practical leather or canvas shoes, no plastic. Something that will form to the foot. Sneakers are a must, more than one pair is good. Could care less about jewelry, unless it is mom's necklace or daddy's watch. Hair styles need to be easy and comfortable. No tight pigtails for the girls or jellied stiff mohawks for the guys. They dress to fit in with the masses rather than stand out.

When a young TWO plays with others, she will always be the mother; rocking the baby, cooking dinner, cleaning the house. She understands that love makes a house a home at a very early age. When a playmate falls, she will quickly help them up and yes, even kiss their boo boo. She is the perfect "little mother". A boy will enjoy playing the loving, caring father. Expect him to play the minister or doctor so he can listen first then make everything better. Both male and female TWOs will love Teddy Bears for the rest of their lives. TWOs are great listeners, better to know your concerns so they may be addressed.

If you are a parent of a TWO you will treasure the ease of raising a small, caring and loving infant. Always keep their sensitive nature in mind when it is time to reprimand them. The use of kind words and compromising solutions will work better than to the loud and abrasive "NO". Help them see your side and they will believe there is a middle where both can agree. Confrontations equal disharmony. An unbalanced TWO will withdraw, sulk and pout. Avoid criticism. Tell your TWO everything she did right followed by a question to allow her to see more possible ways she could have taken action. Bring it from the head back to the heart and she will be fine. During the peer

SEEING KIDS DIFFERENTLY

pressure teenage years she will be the one to encourage her friends to always do the right thing and think of others first labeling her a "goodie two shoes". Keep communication open with your TWO. Adults will find it easy to cross the line with this eager to please child. Help her establish boundaries and teach her "NO" can be a good choice of words when confronted by someone with abusive intentions. Now is the time she will require your support. Urge her to stand her ground.

Group sports are questionable for TWOs. If only they could play a game that always ended in a tie. If someone wins there has to be a loser. It hurts to lose. They don't want to hurt anyone. TWOs are very capable athletes and enjoy solo actives that address their talents; archery, swimming, water skiing, cross fit, rock climbing and biking.

A TWO prefers to stay out of the limelight and yet they have an innate sense of rhythm and balance. So encourage them toward pair or group activities. Father can have her stand on his toes and waltz across the dining room floor or mom can play a duet on the piano with her. For relaxation and imagination get outside and lay on the ground and find figures in the clouds or watch for shooting stars. A TWO will find peace, gratitude and harmony in meditating at any age.

On an off day, the TWO is disagreeable, nit-picky, petty, sly, inconsiderate, disinterested or down right rude. TWOS may appear to be a busybody or supersensitive. A TWO working in the negative will blame others and claim nothing is their fault. She may have bouts of bad temper for trivial reasons. When an illogical mindset is present it may be best just to get out of her way and return later and act like nothing happened.

Other characteristics:

- Find it difficult to decide for fear of picking the wrong answer.
- Often seen as an apple polisher or a brown nosier.
- Say what they think you want to hear rather than the truth.
- Always eager to please everyone, young and old alike.
- Pays great attention to details, small things matter.
- Perfectionist, very determined to make everything all right.
- Plays "follow the leader" without ever being one.

LIFEPATH 2 – MY NURTURING PEACEMAKER

- Fearful of standing alone in the world.
- Never wants to make a mistake or bring attention to herself.
- Dislikes conflicts, but loves to kiss and make up.
- Likes pets, knowing she will always have something to love.
- Not a cry baby, but cries easily when emotionally upset.
- Loves the sunrise and sunset, loves the start and finish.

All in all, your child will maintain a strong healthy life with a well balanced childhood. A TWO child is thin-skinned. By keeping their feelings inside they may not be able to "stomach" everything. They may refuse to eat, suffer from constipation, develop colic or suffer from food allergies. Trouble with communicating will result in sore throats or tonsillitis.

Again, true balance is found in the paths ahead of the TWO and following it. You can teach her to find her own uniqueness, mental strength and trust in self from the vibration of the ONE. When she sees her own strengths the true meaning of cooperation is learned. She can add the emotional joy of attaining harmony and beauty from the number THREE. This will allow her to bring comfort, warmth and affirmation to all the world. This success will create the demand for the TWO's peacemaker skills and knowledge, and fulfill their underlying desire to be needed.

As the second numerological commandment, peace is a strong lesson to learn and enforce. It is important for all Lifepaths to see both sides of an issue. Everyone needs to be still and become balanced.

Whatever becomes of your NURTURING PEACEMAKER my wish is that you are able to recognize her individuality, boost her self-worth and accept her uniqueness.

◄ SEEING KIDS DIFFERENTLY

These TWOs are our future psychologists, police officers, romance novelists, teachers, United Nations representatives, group singers, astrologists, social workers, marriage councilors, geographers, poets and event planners.

_____
_____
_____
_____
_____
_____

> "Before we can make friends with anyone else,
> we must first make friends with our selves."
>
> - Eleanor Roosevelt

Lifepath 3 – My HAPPY GO LUCKY JOY GIVER

Of course this enthusiastic, sparkling, vivacious jester is going to deal with life emotionally. With an open heart wanting true happiness for all the family and many friends this witty new soul will get the job done. Anyone who makes it their life goal to entertain the masses has to be dealing on an emotional level. Amusing others is a release of sensitivity and expression of oneself. This can be very emotional.

Again we see the feminine energy. Not quite as strong as the TWO vibration. Think of what THREE means in Father/Mother/Child. THREE is the child. This little bundle of joy is living in the flow of life. She shares, observes and allows energies to flow in a soft and calm way. She cares about others deeply and her trait this life time is to create love and beauty to lift their spirits.

Your "little Miss Sunshine" will appear to be the social butterfly, interacting with others, talking a lot with little to say, she is still an introvert at heart. She will be the reserved daydreamer with the need for solitude so she may paint, write poetry and connect with nature. Even though her aim is to bring joy to the world not many will know exactly what she is thinking.

An infant THREE will break out of the womb cooing. She is eager to bring a smile to your face, if only with her smile. When it is time to potty train show your joy when a task is completed. If all it takes to make you laugh is sitting on a large cup and showing you what she normally does in private she will quickly master this function. And if eating those green peas and orange carrots makes you just as happy, please fill my bowl.

What to wear? She will pick out her clothes based on her mood for the day. Some days high fashion with everything matching will allow her to strike a pose for others to enjoy. Or today may spark a silly day and she will mismatch socks or wear stripes with flowers to make others laugh. She will enjoy mixing it up. Fill a trunk full of dress up clothes and super hero costumes for when she wants to act the part. She will be drawn to yellow, bright yellow. Full of sunshine, it is a happy, party time color. Be sure she has a full length mirror to view herself prior to making the grand entrance.

In pre-school she will entertain all the other toddlers with her clowning around and silly riddles. Give her a bunch of different hats to take to class. Imagine the thrill she will have in dressing others to perform along with her. She loves toys, lots of them. Keep her creative juices flowing with puppets, legos, masks, coloring books, toy instruments and an Etch a Sketch. Please don't throw away any boxes. You never know what she will do with them with her wild imagination. She will enjoy playing Simon Says. When she is Simon you can't even imagine the different things she will ask others to do. Oh yeah, she will rarely stomp the group, her game is to stay Simon and keep them moving, not give up her post.

As a child it is very important for the THREE's creativity to be recognized, to obtain a sense of acceptance. Praise for completed work will boost her desire to get things done. Encourage understanding the rules with caring disciplinary actions. Try role playing to get a point across. Playing a part will keep her interest and make a point. Her spirit can be broken with strong harsh words and criticism. However she will bounce back quickly. Again part of the show, acting as though it doesn't matter to keep you from feeling guilt, but at the same time hiding her scars. She will always have great energy requiring mental stimulation and diversity.

THREEs are interested in a variety of sports. So many uniforms from which to choose will encourage her to try them all. Although she will enjoy solo activities more where she will be the only one in that particular outfit and the center of attention, joining a team will show off her communication skills and develop responsibility. She will also enjoy inspiring team mates to do their best. Athletics will strengthen her focus and direction, increase her sense of timing and learn discipline. But you can bet your bottom dollar she will be the one in right field catching butterflies or looking for a 4 leaf clover.

You may find your teenage THREE never committing to any cliques. With her personal magnetism she will be attracted to all types to entertain them as she gains insight to what motivates them all. Supply her with a sturdy backpack, not for her books but for all the other gear she will need. A joke book, tickets to a concert or tap dance shoes would make a

LIFEPATH 3 – MY HAPPY GO LUCKY JOY GIVER

wonderful Christmas gift. President of the drama club would give her recognition. You will find her as the lead in the school play, soloist in the choir, playing Wipeout on the drums or voted the class clown. Encourage this performing child with dance lessons, music and voice lessons, art classes, essay contests and writing poetry. After trying a variety she will be drawn to one or two that inspire her dreams of bringing joy to the masses with her personal talent.

Not every one has a perfect life. Somedays it will be difficult to "put on the happy face". Remember to always encourage and listen. Never criticize. To judge or find fault with this happy little charmer is cruel to her spirit. When a THREE has a bad day, vanity will show its weary head. Or her deeply hidden sense of insecurity will be exposed. She will imagine everyone is aware of something she is not. She may expose her self pity. Here is when she will find moral strength in the support from her family, mentor and teachers. Learn the words now to "Put On a Happy Face."

Other characteristics:

- Needs to express her ideas, vision and feelings.
- Displays personal magnetism. Just like Romeo.
- Appreciates art and beauty.
- Loves to train pets to do tricks and then dress them up to preform.
- Born with innate curiosity. You should encourage it.
- Has an optimistic approach to life. No worries.
- Very imaginative. Creates tall tales to entertain friends.
- Exhibits compelling charisma.
- Youthful in thought, will always be a kid young at heart.
- Will procrastinate in picking up toys or doing homework.
- May try their painting skills on the bedroom walls.
- Loves to read novels. May create different endings to some.
- Always at her best, daytime or night time.

Your joy giver will lead a healthy life and have a forever young attitude and great recuperation skills due to her optimism. If your THREE is emotionally upset with life she may display frustrating habits, like biting her nails or lips, constantly clear her throat or breaking out in hives. Her inner tension may cause twitching due to the inability to relax. As a parent or mentor you may need to give her extra attention. THREEs like to be the point of everyone's focus.

SEEING KIDS DIFFERENTLY

As an adult figure in her life you may encourage a balanced life for the THREE by looking to the numbers before and after for growth. She must learn cooperation, flexibility and balance from the TWO. True happiness is found when emotional experiences are shared. She needs to learn to listen to others. However, more will be learned from the FOUR. Teach her stability, organization and understanding limitations. The FOUR will provide all this for the THREE. Learning these traits can build a strong foundation without losing the talent to visualize.

As the third numerological commandment, happiness is what everyone seeks. Joy is vital to all human souls. Laughter cures disease. Music makes the heart sing. Three is a lucky number. You are a lucky parent to have a THREE in your life.

Whatever becomes of your HAPPY GO LUCKY JOY GIVER my wish is that you are able to recognize her individuality, boost her self-worth and accept her uniqueness.

LIFEPATH 3 – MY HAPPY GO LUCKY JOY GIVER

These THREEs are our future Oscar winners, children's book authors, hairstylists, Orchid growers, civil attorneys, portrait artists, architects, horse trainers, jewelry designers, youth counselors, Jazz singers and comedians.

_____
_____
_____
_____
_____
_____
_____

> "It is the supreme art of the teacher to awaken joy in creative expression and knowledge."
>
> - Albert Einstein

Lifepath 4 – My DEVOTED CHILD of the EARTH

This little builder is productive, practical, precise, prepared and "physical". The first response to most actions and emotions will be shown and dealt with on a physical level. A FOUR will use both arms and legs to get to the destination. This child is a mover. Expect him to bounce and rock. You may need to be a bit physical as well. The FOUR loves the be rocked to sleep, play horsey on your leg and walk and run as soon as he is able. He will be very animated as in talking with his hands.

Of course with all this physical action a male vibration is this path's driving force. When you hear someone refer to a child as "all boy" that would most likely be a FOUR. Please don't worry if your FOUR is a girl, just don't expect her to play with dolls and want to grow up to be a princess. I have a friend with two FOUR daughters. He always brags about them being the boys he never had. Tomboys are making headlines these days as star athletes and aggressive CEO where their abilities with structure, consistence and methodical ways will bring any team or company to the top.

Without a doubt, this FOUR who acts first then thinks and talks more than he listens has to be an extrovert. Your little scout will enjoy showing the troops how to blaze a trail, clear the woods, put up a tent and build a fire. This outgoing child enjoys routine. He will take the lead, addressing each task slow and easy and gets it all completed as a job well done.

While in the womb this brand new soul will show his strength and agility with lots of movement. He may react to mom's exercising or loud room noises with a good swift kick of his own. The baby's delivery to this new life was probably quick. This little bundle of energy is determined from the start. As a mover and a shaker he will kick off the covers and find a way to climb out of the crib at a very young age. Potty training will be a challenge. Begin the task with a routine. Allow him to watch you set up the chair, lay out

LIFEPATH 4 – MY DEVOTED CHILD OF THE EARTH

the wipes and powder and have the folded fresh training pants right there. Maybe read a book while he sits, just to keep him sitting. If he sees the order of the task it will appear to be an important job that needs to be completed. Along with mud pies the toddler FOUR will enjoy building his own food. Let him mix his salad, construct the layers of topping on the hamburger and let him pour the gravy in to the mashed potato hole he created. If you serve him ice cream on a cone he will never let it drip and keep it cone shaped on top as he controls the shape as he eats it. A bowl of scooped ice cream will quickly become a block as he chips away mouthfuls with his shovel. He shouldn't have a problem eating any foods as long as he can build it and organize his plate.

Practical clothing is what you want to buy this little worker bee. T-shirts with a breast pocket, cargo shorts with lots of pockets, Levi's so they hold up to the weather, flannel shirts for warmth. Also tie shoes, cross fit sneakers or pull on boots. Little girls will like durable clothes as well. Cotton, loose fitting clothes, jumpers and sweat pants. She will enjoy an apron to keep herself clean and respectable. She will only wear flat soled shoes, no slip ons or flip flops, too easy to lose in the mud. A nice pair of cowboy boots will bring a smile to her face. Even though the FOUR needs to dress in fashion to stay organized and get the task completed he also wants to feel clean and "all put together". The color green will get the job done, as any scout, soldier or Green Bay packer knows. Blues, grays and off whites are also acceptable. Really the FOUR just wants to blend in to the crowd.

Your little helper needs to be organized, establish a plan, gather the best materials in order to complete a solid, secure and stable foundation of any kind. Masons start with blocks, farmers start with shovels and rakes, architects start with puzzles, home builders start with Lincoln Logs, sculptors start with Silly Putty and inventors start with Legos. Your toddler will enjoy throwing a blanket over two dining room chairs just to sit under it and glow in his ability to create a structure. And remember to invest in a piggy bank for him. In school he will love the idea of having his own locker. And will keep his desk organized and pencils sharpened. No need to ask him to help clean up before going out for recess, look around he already did it.

Along with keeping his mind full of creativity, remember to show him system and order. Teach him to follow directions step by step to eliminate jumping ahead to finish fast. Slow and steady wins the race.

SEEING KIDS DIFFERENTLY

The FOUR is well-behaved but lacks kindheartedness. Because your little sand castle builder is so in to structure and knowing his limitations he may find it difficult to express his emotions. He already knows how to live in the box, your challenge will be to get him to see beauty and kindness. Giving compliments and saying thank you just are not part of his way of thinking. But can easily be taught.

The FOUR will attempt many sports. He knows that moving and stretching will keep him fit to get any job done. Running a long distance race, battling it out on the tennis courts, archery, cross country skiing or joining the wrestling team will show off his endurance, strength and obedience. Any sport that calls for the FOUR to be steady and persistent will catch his eye. He wants to do his personal best without seeking the reward of a win.

His lack of imagination and creativity will allow him to have his classmates come up with all the ideas and then give him the pleasure of getting the project completed. He prefers to get a part time job after school like a paper route, stocking shelves at the local hardware store or mowing lawns. He knows the value of working hard to get ahead. The FOUR gets an education through experience rather than schooling. He is also a sensible saver, knows how to handle money and the importance of a bank account. He can be socially awkward, but very well liked. He has a few very close friends. His rigid way of approaching life limits him in exploring other cultures. He is totally not interested in traveling far from home or eating sushi.

Other characteristics:

- Patriotic, likes the red, white and blue even at a young age.
- Knows and understands limitations.
- Expect to hear "Why?' and "What for?" often.
- Loves dirt, sand and rocks.
- Has an excellent memory, especially with numbers.
- The reward is in getting the task completed, never the recognition.
- He would rather blend it to the crowd than stand out in it.
- Tends to be stubborn if he does not understand the rules.
- Will always look up to the strongest one in the family or crowd.
- Is a good communicator, especially in giving instructions.

LIFEPATH 4 – MY DEVOTED CHILD OF THE EARTH

- Really enjoys it when the family gets together to do a project.
- Lacks humor, unless he is playing a practical joke on you.
- Likes the day, he can get a good day's work in under the sun.

Since the FOUR is a physical being, when his day is not going right or he is carrying a lot of weight on his shoulders he will be prone to muscle spasms, cramps and joint pains. A FOUR likes his home to be strong, secure and without chaos, a divorce in the family may cause panic attacks, depression, severe headaches or a total lack of attention which may result in a freak accident. When he pinches a finger or twists an ankle he will walk it off by pacing back and forth. As the pain seizes he will slow down. Teach your child early to relax and enjoy life. He is not responsible for everyone all the time.

FOURS need THREEs in their lives to teach them to lighten up on life, not to see the world only under a magnifying glass. They must bring some joy in to their life through humor and entertainment. FOURS also have to relax, cut loose, learn to be free without losing security. They need to build a gate in the fence that surrounds them. A few FIVEs as friends will share their experiences and teach the FOUR all about change and freedom. When this is accomplished, the FOUR can build success and live in harmony with the limitations he has constructed for himself.

As the fourth numerological commandment, organization is needed to build a strong foundation in order to grow. Everyone needs security, scruples and dependability. The FOUR is here to teach you all of this and more.

Whatever becomes of your DEVOTED CHILD of the EARTH my wish is that you are able to recognize his individuality, boost his self-worth and accept his uniqueness.

◄ **SEEING KIDS DIFFERENTLY**

These FOURs are our future financial advisers, contractors, webpage designers, real estate developers, masons, landscape designers, log home builders, forest rangers, bulldozer operators, chemists, gymnasts and sculptors.

_____
_____
_____
_____
_____
_____
_____
_____

"Productivity is never an accident. It is always the result of a commitment to excellence, intelligent planning and focused effort."

- Paul J. Meyer

Lifepath 5 – My ADVENTURE SEEKER

This little Dora the Explorer will be courageous, versatile, energetic, eager, funny and uplifting. With that description only physical can claim the actions of a FIVE. Be ready for this little daring, inquisitive and flexible traveler to use all five fingers, toes and yes, senses to hunt and seek in all directions.

FIVEs are very unique. They share both male and female instincts. This is the first and only path I will refer to as "they". Freedom has no gender. With four paths before them and four to follow, this little adaptable soul is kind of stuck in the middle making it easy to see the strength and forcefulness of the male as well as the soft and nurturing elements of the female. They have the ability to use their left brain and right brain to analyze the situation and move foreword and upward.

Carl Jung popularized the characteristics of extroverts and introverts. He also claimed there is no such thing as a pure one of either. Your FIVE will have equal traits of both. So let me introduce you to an ambivert. They love to talk, but will also listen. They are enthusiastic and outgoing as well as reserved and solitary. Will easily be distracted but they can also exhibit a strong focus when necessary. I told you the FIVE is a unique human being.

Your baby to be will wiggle in the womb and then burst out with super energy to view and feel this new world of theirs. The FIVE will suck their thumb, sometimes even their toes. Potty training will come easy to them. FIVEs need to be free of restrictions so they will strip away the diapers at first chance. This is an excellent method for training them to relieve themselves appropriately. These little babes will go to any one, any time. A new face, a new voice, and a new smell is like a brand new adventure.

SEEING KIDS DIFFERENTLY

The FIVE will prefer cotton and natural textiles, even silks next to their skin to allow it to breathe. Comfort and accessible movement will keep this little go getter happy. One piece outfits instead of tops and bottoms. Barefoot is the way to go, the more they feel the better. Later they will be attracted to paisleys, odd colors and loud patterns. Also provide them with a huge closet. The FIVE loves variety, needs clothes for whatever occasion is to arise. A closet full of party clothes, travel clothes and athletic clothes with comfortable, yet matching flat or low heeled shoes to match. FIVEs will always be drawn to turquoise. This color is flexible, can be used to dress up or dress down. FIVEs like to accessorize. As many different things to complete an outfit the better.

You will need to keep an eye on this toddler at all times. They are fast, fearless and just need to be free. Their innate sense of adventure will get them in to every thing and a lot of trouble. This little whipper-snapper can make your life an adventure as well. With their curious and motivated nature they will keep you entertained and tired. As the parent of a FIVE feel free to give up your gym membership. Just keeping up with them will keep you fit. Remember to stay one step ahead of them, they will forever be grasping at colorful, bright and usually breakable objects or cutting loose to get away from any make believe confinement. They will enjoy any and all foods. So many colors, tastes and textures. Be sure to tire them out first before attempting to put them in a carseat or even talk about bedtime. Mobiles and colorful moving toys will help to divert attention and allow them to relax. But beware, these little escape artists will easily get out of the crib whenever they want to do so. And the little thrill seeker will feel, smell, listen, taste and examine everything he or she gets their hands on. A FIVE is easily bored, so make sure to entertain them with toys, books, crafts and movies.

As an ambivert they will swing between "let me go" and "help me" in an instant. Understanding this will make discipline a challenge. You need to introduce structure in to their lives early on. Timeouts are good if not too long. Do anything to slow them down and allow them to see their intentions. "Hold on there, where are you going and what do you think you are doing?" Give them time to think and express themselves at a young age and continue with this tactic through adulthood. They will display their sensuality at a very young age. Remember they are born to deal with all five senses. If something feels good they will do it. So if your FIVE takes to pleasure touching him or herself, let them know it is okay to do so at home only and in the privacy of their own room. Understand your child needs to learn by doing, with trial and error. In order to keep your FIVE enthusiastic you will be required to be alert and progressive. Show them how broadminded you are about every thing to keep them interested in you. This will always keep communication open.

Sports are interesting because they create activity, but following the rules or better yet the leader will prove to be a challenge. Show them a sport that allows them to live without barriers and you will find a winner. Freestyle sports like snowboarding, roller skating or surfing are more appealing to the daring, agile, flexible FIVE. Motorbiking, cross fit training, ski jumping, sky diving and rock climbing will evoke the thrill of it all in this adrenalin junkie. Hiking, wilderness camping and survival training will excite this wandering adventure seeker with the challenge of the great outdoors. FIVEs are the wild kids.

Teachers will view FIVEs as underachievers due to their appeared lack of focus. When the challenge is over, the FIVE is out of here. With their eagerness to know and understand they will want to be friends with everyone in the class. One day they will hang with the academic crowd to see what they know that he or she doesn't. Tomorrow the athletic teens will look exciting and carefree. Even the special ed class will provide an insight to a different way of life. Next day the FIVE will cut class. In high school the FIVE is the life of the party and will try anything once. Educate them early on the rules, responsibilities and punishments of sex, drugs and rock and roll. It is extremely important to keep communication alive in regards to pleasures of this sort. Understand right now that FIVEs learn with experience and not rules. But trust in the fact that they won't stick to any thing very long. Their desire for constant change will keep them moving on to more rewarding activities. Take them on an adventuresome road trip, buy them a new action video game, get them involved with a new fast moving exciting sport. Lure them in the next direction with a change of scenery and a brand new challenge.

Other characteristics:

- Lots of foot tapping, knuckle cracking or nail biting.
- Experience is the best teacher.
- Many sided, has the ability to do many different things at once.
- Great at procrastinating.
- Will touch a stove just to see if it is hot.
- Likes the eccentrics and misfits of society.

- Never sweats the small stuff.
- Saves money to travel.
- Enjoys the change of seasons.
- Knows no limits.
- Has no attraction to clubs, groups, cults or religions.
- Has many unconventional and different talents and hobbies.
- Sees the challenges and adventures of both day and night.

The free spirit FIVE is normally healthy throughout their entire life. However, negative thoughts and often unwarranted challenges will create dis-ease in both mental and physical areas. They may be pessimistic, have temper tantrums or won't be able to sleep. Or they may battle stammering or suffer with earaches. Absent minded the FIVE may be accident prone and any cuts can easily become infected.

For a FIVE to reach their full potential they need to experience freedom constructively. Help your child to become organized in manner and thought like the FOUR. Teach them about living in the box for they already know how to live out of it. And the SIX can show them to be supportive of others and how to be responsibility for their quick and sometimes dangerous actions.

As the fifth numerological commandment, freedom is a fun and adventurous lesson. To accept change and welcome challenges is a feat to some, but not to the FIVE.

Whatever becomes of your ADVENTURE SEEKER my wish is that you are able to recognize their individuality, boost their self-worth and accept his or her uniqueness.

LIFEPATH 5 – MY ADVENTURE SEEKER

These FIVEs are our future Mt. Everest climbers, stunt drivers, tightrope walkers, entrepreneurs, scientists, travel blog writers, NASCAR racers, entertainers, motivational speakers, booking agents, locomotive engineers, bartenders or gourmet chefs.

(Your FIVE may have every one of these careers in a lifetime.)

_____
_____
_____
_____
_____
_____
_____
_____

"Conformity is the jailer of freedom and
the enemy of growth."

- John F. Kennedy

Lifepath 6 – My SOFT-HEARTED LOVE CHILD

It is impossible to be soft-hearted and not work with an emotional vibration. Yes, this little SIX made in heaven will have a life of making sure the family, neighbors and classmates are happy and contend. Harmony requires that someone achieve and maintain it in this community, in this world. That someone is your tiny SIX. This bundle of love will make it her responsibility. A huge task to take on for such a caring and accommodating child. Compassion is a very emotional virtue.

This mother of all mothers is working with a female energy. So if you have a tender little boy you may call him the father of all fathers as long as you realize he will be using a gentle, devoting energy to support his kindness and love, not the strong, domineering energy with which you believe a male child is born. In today's world love and harmony is greatly needed. We need every SIX we can create for our next generation to develop our peaceful world of the future.

Yes, this peace loving flower child is an extrovert, with loads of people in her immediate coterie. She was born to develop a circle that will never be broken, only full of love. She needs to be able to approach others easily to make friends, to be supportive of their dreams. She was put on earth to solve everyone's problems. Only an outgoing, talkative, energetic extrovert can accomplish that in one lifetime.

This gentle, quiet baby was most likely gentle and quiet in utero. She made your delivery as easy as possible and cried very little as she made her great entrance. SIX newborns are often described as perfect babies. They are so easy! Remember all she wants to do is please everyone. She will easily go down for a nap and sleep through the night. Expect her to coo and show her dimples for all to see. She will potty train herself, early I may add. And consume and enjoy anything you feed her. After all, SIXs are born to please. She will respond

LIFEPATH 6 – MY SOFT-HEARTED LOVE CHILD

well to lullabies and swaying. And don't forget to tuck her in tight. SIXs love to feel secure, especially as an infant.

It is obvious at this point that all God's little creations want to be dressed for comfort. SIXs are no different. The regular soft cotton polo shirts, jeans, skirts and soft sweaters will suit them just fine. Just make sure all is bright and clean, no stains, patches or worn spots. The SIX is required to look smart and put together at all times. How can you expect her to heal the problems of the neighborhood if she doesn't dress the part? An apron may be a good purchase. At least you will show that you understand her mission. And a backpack or large canvas bag in which she can carry all the stuff she needs to get her daily job completed. She will enjoy sneakers the best. In the summer, sandals that will stay on her feet. You see she may have to capture a run away toddler chasing a ball in to the street. Rain and snow boots are high on the list for school shopping. Ponytails fixed with nice ornaments or colorful barrettes to pull back her hair and short crewcuts for the boys. No deed to fuss with hair when their are problems to solve. The SIX always needs to look well groomed so others will treat her with the respect that is required for a conscientious creature of balance and justice. Indigo may be her favorite color, but primrose and pale blue will always look the part, too.

When it is time to go to school the SIX will glow with the opportunity to meet others. She will come to the aid of her teacher with her ability to calm the others, cope with this new experience and keep order in the classroom. The SIX will be the quiet, mature one in school, setting a good example for the others. She will carry extra tissues, tie many shoes and return a lost book to the rightful owner. The SIX would cherish siblings, she would make the perfect mommy's little helper. If another wants her toy they may have it. Doesn't understand the word "mine". She will forfeit her turn in line for the chance to swing or give up her bike to some child without one. A SIX is always ready to play house. She will dress her baby dolls in warm outfits, rock them to sleep and feed them. SIXs are also known to dress up pets and try to get them in a stroller for a walk. She will be advanced in her class in reading and vocabulary. She loves to read to others and needs to get her point across whenever necessary. Feel free to ask the SIX to help around the house with any chores. They are eager to do the dishes, sweep the porch, fold the laundry, wash the car and make the bed.

She may be going overboard with all this protectiveness. She needs to learn to ask if someone needs her help. Bring to her attention that others have opinions and obligations of their own. She needs to respect the actions others may take that are different from her way of

SEEING KIDS DIFFERENTLY

doing things. If you see your SIX is intrusive and meddling with others, please do your best to explain with example why this is wrong. If you reprimand her with harsh words and in the presence of others it may appear she has taken it all in strait but in reality she will suffer quietly, alone in her room, with a broken spirit. The sentimental SIX is often mistakenly understood. As much as she wants to give love, she also wants to feel loved.

The SIX will enjoy team sports, any team will do. But preferably one that won't get her uniform too dirty. She just wants to feel part of a group that may need her help. She can bandage wounds or console others through the heart ship of a lost. The SIX will be comfortable on the bench. SIXs like activity. She will enjoy a nice bike ride in the park, rollerblading thorough the playground or hiking to the top of a mountain so she may see the peace and tranquility of the earth below.

The SIX feels she is always in control of any disharmony. The SIX will never start an argument, but will be up front and present to mediate one. She will stand up to the bullying of another weaker classmate, but the SIX with her sacrificing nature will allow the name calling, trampling and emotional abused when directed at her. As a parent or school counselor it will be important for you to keep a strong line of communication open with a SIX regarding this subject. Enrolling the SIX in music classes or encouraging her to try out for school plays will allow her beauty to reign. She will enjoy entertaining and her love of the arts will shine. The SIX will take on a part time job in school, like bagging groceries or cleaning for the elderly next door neighbor. But she will be more prone to volunteer at the local animal shelter or candy stripe at a nursing home. If you what to give her a special birthday gift, redecorate her bedroom. However, allow her to organize her own celebration. She can always create the best theme, delicious food and family style games for all to enjoy.

If their is an argument between parents, or God forbid a divorce, the SIX will do everything possible to pacify and plan a truce that will make it all better. It is times like this when SIXs take on too much for the soul. If she can't fix it, what then? Her responsible traits will fail her, her siblings and her parents. Again communication is the answer. Please what ever you do as separating parents do not share your disappointment in your spouse with a SIX. It will be easier if both parties take the blame.

LIFEPATH 6 – MY SOFT-HEARTED LOVE CHILD

Other characteristics:

- Can be very demanding.
- Please don't tell her what to do.
- Praise of a job well done will encourage her to take on a new task.
- Loves to be of service.
- A born manipulator.
- Can see the bigger picture for others when they don't.
- Artistic, with an excellent sense of color.
- May be fussy or trivial at times.
- Very affectionate. Loves to cuddle, kiss and hold hands.
- Remember to say Thank You to a SIX.
- Needs to be loved, wanted and truly respected.
- Never use a "devil may care" attitude around a SIX.
- Likes daytime better, easier to see the beauty.

Although a normally healthy child when she feels out of control may suffer from a stuffy nose or sore throat. Her inability to be heard may cause shortness of breathe. If emotionally upset the child is prone to pant wetting. May also suffer from upset stomach or cramps.

To balance the SIX teach her freedom, let her get a bit wild in a pool or on the playground. Help her except change and show her it can be good to experience a new challenge just like a FIVE does. And involve them in the mysteries of life and investigate them with her like a SEVEN would. This will help when a SIX is judgmental. The balance will result in a stronger, wiser child of love.

As the sixth numerological commandment, responsibility just raises the ladder. If you can teach your child loyalty, devotion and harmony this world will be a better place to live for all of us.

Whatever becomes of your SOFT-HEARTED LOVE CHILD my wish is that you are able to recognize her individuality, boost her self-worth and accept her uniqueness.

◄ SEEING KIDS DIFFERENTLY

These SIXs are our future civil servants, zookeepers, youth group leaders, nuns, Scout leaders, event coordinators, fashion designers, hospital personnel, hairstylists, bartenders, postal clerks and romance novelists.

_____
_____
_____
_____
_____
_____
_____

> "We are made wise not by the recollection of the past,
> but by the responsibility for our future."
> — George Bernard Shaw

Lifepath 7 – My MYSTICAL VISIONARY

With a title like that, this child can only be intuitive. Your child was born with a skill everyone would love to have, the conscious ability to "know". This enlightened soul was gifted with the innate condition to understand truth. Unlike those dealing with mental and physical attributes, which everyone can grasp, your little Merlin will need to follow a path only he controls. And he will have a lifetime of just that.

Yes, he was born with a male vibration. This will give him the secure, enabling energy to handle all this universal power. Also the left brain logic will balance the pull of the opposite forces that will present themselves through out his life. A SEVEN needs to be strong, competitive and aggressive. All prominent male qualities. If your infant SEVEN is a girl just be grateful for this confident energy. She will relish it.

Of course he is an introvert. He will need alone time to think. And this little fellow of yours will be taking a lot of solitary thought breaks. He will need to listen and focus as well. Take it all in so when he has an "I got it" moment he can share it with others. And he needs to handle any and all problems on his own. Do you understand that mom?

I have a feeling your new little bundle of joy knew exactly where he was going when he arrived in your arms at the hospital. It is my belief SEVENs are all returning to complete an internal mission. One that will answer so many questions for this spirit. He was probably gentle in the womb. Quiet with anticipation of this new life a head of him. Could you look deep in to his eyes at birth? Just as though there was a story to be told in them. He can feel your emotions. Even though he can't talk yet, he will try to comfort you when you are sad. Don't expect this tiny angel to cry very much. If he does, check on him. He will only cry for a good reason. When it is time to potty train you will need to explain both options to him. Does he want to sit in a wet diaper or relieve himself in the john and move on in comfort?

SEEING KIDS DIFFERENTLY

After several opportunities to make the right choice, as he sits in privacy, he will be trained. And when you are introducing him to new foods, like a banana, tell him it is a sweet fruit with a mushy, slimy feel on your tongue. Don't just put a spoonful in his mouth and surprise him. He wants to know what you intend to shovel in his mouth before hand. He will be happy where ever he is, in a high chair, a carseat, in the crib, just as long as he can see and hear everything that is going on. Remember timeouts for the SEVEN is never a punishment.

Again soft fabrics rule for the SEVEN. As long as what he has next to is body feels good he really doesn't care what it looks like or how he looks in it. You may dress him any way you like. He may be annoyed by labels on the neckline or a tight spot here or there. There is no need to pick out his style for him. After he grows up a little bit he will try different styles and then pick the one that fits him. If he chooses to be an outdoorsmen he will go for cargo pants and hoodies, if he becomes athletic, sweatpants and T-shirts, a bookworm and he will wear whatever he has to curl up and become absorbed. Footwear abides by the same rules… comfort. He will shy from fads for he knows they won't last. He will be drawn to the spiritual color of violet or any shade of purple. Yellow and shades of brown will also do.

Now he is getting older, he walks, talks and continues to think. You know how I said he was born knowing truth, well at this age he will challenge you with it. "Why is the sky blue?" "How does the TV work?" Be prepared. He will be constantly asking questions that are difficult to answer. Most children ask easy questions, not the SEVEN, he already knows those answers. He now is introduced to so many earthly things that just do not make sense. The little sneaker will always be out of sight, but within voice range. He is very interested in hearing everything that is going on. Not in a malice way, this seeker of truth is purely interested in the thoughts of adults. Other children's thought are too easy and free flowing. He needs to analyze the grown ups, for they must know something more than he does. Other kids won't understand him. He doesn't lead, create or mingle with them. So they pretty much just leave each other alone.

As a parent you may question this young visionary's ability to succeed in life. How can I help him come out of his shell? Again depend on communication. The SEVEN will not be threatened by the middle of the road mentality. Be super casual with your talks so he won't feel any threat. Don't be direct and in your face with questions or lallygag with stupid ones. Introduce a topic and then let him take over. A listener will want someone to listen to him at times. He also needs you to be his security blanket. If he has a question that even he has no answer for it would be nice if he had a parent or another adult figure to go to for advice. Wouldn't it be nice if he came to you?

Endurance sports will get him going and going and going. When totally exhausted he can go home and get some much needed sleep. Cross-country running, mountain biking or even weight lifting may interest him. He has the analytical mind to master the game of football, but would rather use these skills to shout "stale mate".

During his teenager years he will master smartphones and computers with ease. Buy a SEVEN a top of the line camera and you will be amazed in his ability to use the options and software to create masterful landscape photos. Honor him with an enlarged, framed print that claims a spot above the fireplace. This is also a great time to introduce him to stringed musical instruments, like the harp or cello. The mystic in him will daydream he is communicated with the cosmos. In school he will excel in science and history, one needs proof and the other needs to be studied. The SEVEN becomes a loner early in life and then after years of philosophical thought will spread his wings and fly. At any time your sedentary analyzer will come out of his cocoon to make a statement of his own. That may be in high school or college. He may dress up in formal wear on an ordinary school day or dress down in rags for the prom. He may get numerous piecings and tattoos, live a Bohemian life style or join a hard rock band. He may even test the drug scene out. At this stage in life he thinks if he can't join them, why not beat them. Don't worry it will be short lived. It will only be a matter of time before he "knows" this is not who he is.

Loners are challenged by feelings of vulnerability, frustration and alienation from others. Your child may feel like there is no place that he fits in this society. He may feel betrayed at times. On down days the SEVEN will be cold-hearted, cruel, arrogant and verbally abusive. The SEVEN needs a belief system. I am not talking organized religion, however it could be a start. Your seeker of truth needs the answers. It may come from God, a guru, the Dalai Lama or a discipline, like yoga or meditation. His life this time is an internal journey. When he can answer the life long questions, "Who am I?" and "What is my purpose in life?", the thinker will be emancipated.

SEEING KIDS DIFFERENTLY

Other characteristics:

- Has penetrating eyes.
- Can read between the lines.
- A natural born psychic.
- Will never wear a uniform.
- Has a dry sense of humor, can't even remember a joke.
- Good at hiding emotions.
- Favorite saying, "Nothing is exactly as it seems".
- Stays away from crowds.
- Hates drama, it is too short lived.
- Enjoys the company of eccentric and unpopular people.
- Loves ancient ruins and historical museums.
- Likes to wear a mask or role play, be different for a day.
- Enjoys dreaming, so prefers the nights.

The SEVEN knows the importance of rest and intuition will allow him to feel his body. These two elements will keep him healthy through out his lifetime. But if melancholy, suppression and betrayal sets in you may see this child suffer from anxiety and stress. Their bodies become frail and a bicycle fall may break a bone. Acne, hives or a rash may break out when something gets under their skin. Perspiration, night sweats and body odor are apparent if forced to hold too much inside. Lack of truth may leave him hungary and the SEVEN may lose weight to a point of it being unhealthy.

If the SEVEN can learn love and peace from the SIX as well as power and confidence from the EIGHT there is no stopping this dignified, proud, astute intellect who just found faith in himself. Once he finds it he is proud to share it with other to create a better universe.

As the seventh numerological commandment, faith is what teaches us right and wrong. Teach your SEVEN to trust his natural born instincts and encourage him to follow his intuition and use both talents to conquer this world.

Whatever becomes of your MYSTICAL VISIONARY my wish is that you are able to recognize his individuality, boost his self-worth and accept his uniqueness.

LIFEPATH 7 – MY MYSTICAL VISIONARY

These SEVENs are our future scientists, astronauts, librarians, underwater researchers, poets, CIA agents, navigators, computer technicians, day traders, magicians, astrologists and nature photographers.

___

"Faith in oneself is the best and safest course."

- Michelangelo

Lifepath 8 – My DYNAMIC ACHIEVER

With a label like this, your EIGHT can only be working on a mental level. No emotions will ever slow this little golden boy down. His logic, focus and persuasive abilities will enable him to become the successful leader he was meant to be.

If your little director is a female you can expect a "catwoman" to be sharing your home. Yes this powerful high-flyer can only be performing stunts like she does with strong male vibrations. EIGHT's controlling, aggressive, competitive and purpose driven nature can only be achieved with a male energy base.

Since the boss requires an outgoing personality, energetic actions and ability to make impulsive decisions you can be glad this EIGHT is an extrovert. He was born to be king and he will be forthright in his display of proving just that with his ability to lead the commoners.

I bet mom was ready to deliver this little wiggler and kicker. From the day of conception this little guy was ready to move the world. And he was ready to make his grand appearance in the delivery room as well. I bet it was loud. EIGHTs love attention and when you can't do much else, you scream! This little ruler will start his path at a very young age. The EIGHT baby will be quick, so keep an eye on him. He will be tight lipped to feed, unless he loves what you are spooning him. He will grab at all and anything he can and push everything that doesn't appeal to him away. Sometimes it may be you. Don't expect to hold and cuddle this little dynamo, the EIGHT will not be held down. And when it comes to potty training, he may show you how it is done. He is the commander in every way.

The EIGHT will like to dress the part. A paper crown from Wendy's will make his day. The right clothes will stay on this child. As long as he looks important it doesn't matter if its comfortable. Feel free to dress the EIGHT up. A hat, tie and vest with tied on hard leather

LIFEPATH 8 – MY DYNAMIC ACHIEVER

dress shoes will make him appear to others that he means business. Now I wouldn't do this on a daily bases, but when you do, know that he appreciates your effort in helping the monarch rule his kingdom. Later, when he picks out his own clothes he will choose quality, name brand items that cost a pretty penny. Young ladies will be drawn to pant suits. The EIGHT will adore shoes. Just the right pair will always make a statement. Gray, dark browns and navy will get people to follow him, but pink will make a lasting impression.

Oh boy, the toddler years. This little fireball can not be stopped. Try to and you may be in for the tantrum of all tantrums! The EIGHT was born in to this lifetime to make it big. Try to even slow him down and you will see his angry side. I suggest a dog leash when out in the public arena. I know it sounds gruel or embracing for you, but does a run away lost child or a screaming lunatic sound better? If you need to restrain the EIGHT make sure you divert his attention first. Have his favorite juice, toy or DVD on hand before clipping him into a carseat or stroller. He will be the hero or rescuer for any other siblings or classmates. EIGHTS will be willing to save all others that show up in his young life. How's that for displaying control of a situation. "Come along and follow me." He will enjoy toys that move. You won't need training wheels on this fellow's first two wheeler. Anything with wheels will keep him entertained. The faster and more noise the better. Race cars are great, their speed will fascinate him. However trucks have a purpose, they are designed to get the job done. He will enjoy blocks, the higher he can tower them the better. His toys will reflex the way his mind works.

Believe it or not, the little rebel rouser is looking for discipline. Handling and harnessing this power is the same question he has had on his mind since birth. He chose the two of you as parents and teachers. You may need to loyally enforce timeouts with the young EIGHT. After so many bouts of door slamming and shouting, the required alone time to enable him to think will allow the EIGHT to be able to reason with you. Prepare yourself for his outbursts. Catch them before they totally develop then start a reasoning conversation with him. Teaching him to be the CEO someday means he needs to "mind" his superiors at a young age. He is looking for leadership role models. When you reprimand the EIGHT do it face to face at an equal level. Do not stand over him and yell. Address the problem calmly with him on his mental level. If he stares back in to your eyes confidently you know he is space banking this power logically for future use of your talents to get his well deserved attention from the masses later in life. Be strong and decisive with patience and kindness. This may take time and perseverance, another mentoring trait. Don't forget about money. Have him set up a

SEEING KIDS DIFFERENTLY

lemonade stand on the corner. Easy money for any child. Share with him how you make your money, how to use it wisely or save it for the future. And more importantly how to share it generously with others. The sign for infinity is the figure eight lying on its side. It represents the infinite motion of what goes around comes around. Your financier has the ability to make a fortune. If he learns early on in life that he is the force that keeps this ever moving energy, called money, alive he can obtain the highest level of personal power. Show the EIGHT the value of money early and he will prosper in more ways then you will ever imagine.

EIGHTs love, love, love sports. He will try them all so he may show his strength, endurance, competitiveness and keep himself focused on results. In sports the EIGHT will learn unwavering discipline and clear boundaries. Any team sport will show this captain leadership. Expect them to retire his number someday. The EIGHT will be the team's home run hitter, most points ever scored in a season of basketball or be the youngest golfer to play in the Masters. He is a born Hall Of Fame athlete. In bed at night he will visualize scoring big and the next day he will do just that.

If you did your job as a parent your well developed EIGHT will be the BMOC (Big Man on Campus) in high school and college. His industrious ability and upright personality will allow him to fit in to any clique. He will be "real" and show street smarts so others will follow him to learn how he does it. High school peers will all want him in their group. He will be a good judge of character and always choose the right friends. The EIGHT is academical intelligent. He will be busy as the class president, sports star and with his commissioned based after school job. The commission will develop character building and hold his interest, besides grant him a huge paycheck. And oh yeah, buy him a really good helmet for his motorcycle.

The EIGHT will always have the "I can do it better" attitude. This is fine and dandy if this statement is a personal desire and ends with the words "than last time" verses "than you". Bossy, blunt and too direct is using his power incorrectly. The EIGHT will have struggles with authority and need to break the rules. Some EIGHTS will show greediness or worse, become a bully. They will be constantly challenged to respect other lifepath's individual traits and talents. It can be difficult for this powerhouse to accept shyness, nurturing, soft or sympathetic ways of others. Feelings deep in the heart are so foreign to the EIGHT's nature. Negative attributes show up as insensitive, cruel, unscrupulous and ruthless. Or they may feel like a victim of circumstances and withdraw in depression.

LIFEPATH 8 – MY DYNAMIC ACHIEVER

Other Characteristics:

- Honest to a fault. He will never show a talent for fibbing.
- Should view money as tool with which to grow.
- Is a risk taker and little daredevil.
- Has the drive to overcome any obstacles.
- Likes to help others see their dreams come true.
- Don't expect flowers or candy as gifts. Too sentimental.
- Appreciates art and music, but no desire to create it himself.
- Needs to enjoy daily exercise.
- Will be attracted to older folks, wants to grow wise like them.
- Intense energy for his entire life.
- Will push boundaries to their limit.
- Needs to be a leader, so you may want to pretend to follow him.
- Likes the night, gives him control of a different type of power.

The power and strength of the EIGHT will offer them a healthy life that grows with age. Studies show many centurions are EIGHTS. A nervous child will annoy you with his knuckle cracking. Stressful days will cause allergies, laryngitis and warts. If the EIGHT finds it difficult to take it all in, you may find him susceptible to asthma.

To keep the EIGHT flowing evenly, he must learn when to be quiet and reflect on the day from the SEVEN path. To be still and relaxed. The peaceful and softer nature of the NINE path will teach him to achieve power of the heart, not just the mind. This well adjusted realist will have all of humanity following his lead to make this a perfect world.

As the eighth numerological commandment, leadership puts us all in the right direction. If you can teach your child personal power that shows in his kindness and consideration of others we can all expect to live in a world of high standards, with ethics and abundance.

Whatever becomes of your DYNAMIC ACHIEVER my wish is that you are able to recognize his individuality, boost his self-worth and accept his uniqueness.

◄ **SEEING KIDS DIFFERENTLY**

These EIGHTs are our future criminal experts, bankers, philosophers, real estate developers, stock brokers, insurance agents, managers of professional sport teams, fortune 500 leaders, forensic investigators, government officials, antique dealers and Time magazine editors.

_____
_____
_____
_____
_____
_____
_____

"If your actions inspire others to dream more,
learn more and become more, you are a leader."

- John Quincy Adams

Lifepath 9 – My OLD SOUL HEALER

This merciful, chivalrous and noble child of God can only be doing these incredible deeds through intuition. Every soul arrives on earth with a 'knowing" that can only come from one source. Your small being arrived surrounded by this energy. Your old soul NINE will live this lifetime displaying intuitive abilities to everyone's amazement. Truth be told, not all others encountered will understand this energy, but will be drawn to every action and word out of the NINE's mouth.

NINEs are nurturing, engaging and flowing. Only a feminine energy can pull off those traits. She will take you in, her magnetism will envelop your senses, you will feel perfect in her presence. A woman's intuition is said to come from the gut. It may come across as a psychic ability. Trust wishing on your star and know that she will open your eyes.

She will listen to your every word, appear reserved and approachable by all. The master introvert will capture you with her quietness and solitary ways, knowing full well the NINE has so much to say and teach you.

You just gave birth to a teacher. It starts from day one you know. Your NINE allowed you to experience the perfect birthing ritual. It may have started from conception. Your pregnancy went completely as planned. Did you see her aura on first glance? You know the glow that surrounded her entire body. I hope you took it in, rather than shed it away in "your" excitement. The birth of a NINE is altruistic. I hope you didn't miss it. This infant is like no other. You can feel her love for you as you cradle the NINE in your arms. When others hold her they won't want to give her back. The little angel will love to be touched, love splashing in the tub, having her diaper changed and being rocked to sleep. She is easy to potty train and takes whatever food you suggest she eats. The NINE is fully aware that all this is making you a delightful parent.

SEEING KIDS DIFFERENTLY

Are you familiar with a child that just strips themselves of any restraints to allow them to be free? You know the one who undresses for no reason and flutters around like a just released butterfly. That is your NINE. Understand she is really showing you how to let go. But until you learn try all the pastels in all natural fabrics with no tight areas. NINEs desire to be warm, physically, mentally and emotionally. Later she will enjoy scarlet or crimson, the color of the heart. Your NINE will literally wear her heart on her sleeve. Shoes? Again barefooted will please her, but all cotton or wool slippers will keep her protected and warm.

As an old soul she may miss the toddler stage of growth. And the teenage century as well. But I have made it my goal to teach parents to understand their children with my insights of the numbers so bear with me. The path of the NINE is to live this life with all the previous individual path's uniquenesses. The wise NINE will show you all the talents and traits of paths one through eight. She is Godlike. A master of all life. So if you describe her talents as one that you either portray or lack, know that she wants you to "see" this in yourself and glorify it or let it go.

That being said, your toddler may not relate to others her age. On the playground this NINE will mirror other children's actions in a way to address their weaknesses in hopes they understand and improve now while they are still young. If a playmate stresses over getting mud on her shoes, the NINE will dirty her own shoes and after also declaring her shoes to be muddy will go to the fountain and wash the mud off. So simple, but yet in your face. Don't worry, your born do-gooder will grow into a more kinder counselor as she approaches the teenage years. However the NINE will always prevail with provoking questions and insightful observations. Your precocious child will come well equipped with excellent manners and well-intentioned motives that will appease the surrounding witnesses. This little St. Francis of Assisi has a close connection to all animals. One of my childhood NINE friends once climbed a farmer's fence to rescue a calf from becoming veal. He lassoed it with his belt and took it home to his mom, claimed the baby cow just followed him there. And other NINEs have the ability to train birds to eat from their palms and turn feral kittens in to adoring pets.

How do you begin to train a child with a NINE path? When she is really here to train you. Love her in every way possible. Read her the classic fairytales where love wins all and lessoned are learned. Encourage her charitable ways by allowing her to give dollars to the homeless and throw coins in the plastic "please help" boxes on the store counters. When

LIFEPATH 9 – MY OLD SOUL HEALER

you bring any selfish move or bad behavior to the NINE's attention, do so with dignity and speaking to them at an adult level. Chances are she will apologize profusely and promise never, ever to do it again. And then you can spend some solitary moments giving thought to what she is trying to make you see within yourself. The sharing of this awakening moment with your born philosopher will brighten her day.

Sports are inviting to the NINE. And she will excel in any she attempts. Acrobatics, fencing, karate, skeet shooting, tennis, mountain motorbiking…if you are interested in the sport, so is she. The NINE aims to allow you to live thorough her athletic abilities.

Expect the artists in the NINE to drag you to the latest gallery opening, the new opera in the city or a Shakespearean play in the park. Her culture will explode in high school and college. Her love for the arts will be recognized and released. This well intentioned teenager will follow her hunches, be attuned to her gut feelings and revealing her intuitive abilities in order to prove she is a friend to all by knowing her classmates thoughts. Years later, at the 20th year class reunion she will be mentioned as the one who made a difference in all their lives. She makes friends easily and keeps them close. NINES will always be well groomed and in style, with the enhancing dress lines, tailored Oxford shirts, pressed seams and polished shoes, tastefully styled with a matching scarf and dainty jewels. She will never adorn her body with items made by child labor.

If challenged in any way it may be the NINE chose this path prematurely. To realize that their goals this path have proven to be more difficult than aspired can leave your child feel they are not of this world and prefer not to stay. Or you may have not shown your ability to heed their directions and release those weights that continue to hold you down. Your young care giver will view her life as a failure to achieve her path of goodness and love. This can cause depression and soul felt melancholy. Your NINE may avoid asking for help. And their compassion for others may turn on them and end up being taken advantage of by people thought to be friends. Your NINE may become impersonal, egocentric, cold, arrogant or fickle. Teens may try to buck the system if they think they can.

Other characteristics:

- A daydreamer. Off on some adventure in a different galaxy.
- A true giver in every way.

SEEING KIDS DIFFERENTLY

- In complete control of the situation without becoming a leader.
- Knows that things can get worse before getting better.
- Keeps promises.
- Often asks questions for which they know the answers.
- May get lost in the woods while getting in touch with nature.
- Most conscious and tolerant and least judgmental of others.
- Chooses to loves all rather than only one.
- Believes in a perfect world with a happy ending.
- "Bighearted"
- Is accepting of death for they know it is part of life.
- Best at night, less noticeable imperfections in the dark.

The NINEs intuition will keep her body healthy throughout her long lived life. It is the distractions and her getting lost in her thoughts that will make her accident prone. Stitches, bruises and broken bones will keep her pediatrician busy, not illnesses.

Once again, the NINE will find balance from below and above. From the EIGHT she can capture the even and steady flow of life, while allowing to let go and lead as the ONE has achieved. Knowing and trusting this the NINE will create a complete world full of God power and love of all mankind.

As the ninth numerological commandment, completion tells us the story of life. And the moral is to trust your intuition. If you can teach your NINE to rely on her God given talents and trust her gut feelings to encourage her to show the way to others we can expect to soon be living in utopia.

Whatever becomes of your OLD SOUL HEALER my wish is that you are able to recognize her individuality, boost her self-worth and accept her uniqueness.

LIFEPATH 9 – MY OLD SOUL HEALER

These NINEs are our future Nobel Peace Prize winners, life coaches, Red Cross volunteers, abstract artists, media broadcasters, Sec. of States, firefighters, builders of non-profit organizations, medical missionaries, publishers, veterinarians and Blues musicians.

_____
_____
_____
_____
_____
_____
_____
_____

> "Some people say there's nothing new under the sun.
> I still think that there's room to create, you know.
> And intuition doesn't necessarily come from under the sun.
> It comes from within."
>
> — Pharrell Williams

Using Your "Sight"

Well, how did I do in describing your child? My hope for you is that you better understand your children and the force of their individual paths. I want you to keep this book handy until the children graduate from high school. Not all talents and traits will be apparent at all times. Each soul goes through various stages. My insights were written to allow you to know who your child is from the inside out. The child is more free to be themselves at a younger age. As they mature they start putting on masks for the benefit of parents and friends. I hope you will allow your offspring to be who they are every year they are under your care. And to know them well enough to guide them through the peer pressure years. They will probably fend for themselves through the next 4 decades. Then we reach an age when we return to what we believe we are truly meant to be. Ask any grandparent.

Please use this knowledge to create a happier and healthier life for your entire family. You should be able to recognize each child for what they bring to the table, the dinner table that is. The evening meal is a great time to share and communicate. Bring back this family tradition. Start each dinner with a compliment, acknowledge accomplishments, give them each a sense of importance, encourage individual growth, show them respect for decisions that made their day and they will grow up knowing they are loved. Include both parents during this exercise. Moms and Dads need to be part of this group sharing. Learn not to critically question their actions or try to change them in any way. As children of the next millennium they will all have peaceful, nurturing attributes. Allow them to practice with family pay-it-forward missions and the joy of volunteering. And most of all, teach them to share their gratitude. I grew up with the Lord's Prayer. I suggest you use a more modern technique. Starting and ending each day with a statement of thanks is a great idea. "I am thankful for the snow that fell last night." "I am thankful for the A I received in school today." "I am thankful for those wonderful cookies you baked today." And instead of using a generic "thank you" with others, get them accustomed to answering with, "I am thankful you just did that for me." Or "I love this. I am so thankful for your special gift." And lastly, introduce the family early on to the importance of group family hugs. Growing up in a German culture, I really missed the loving, familiar touch of a hug.

If you read all the children's life path descriptions you may have caught several mentions of the word "stress". Yes, many children feel stress as they grow up. There is no physical pain with your child's inner pressures so they may not share them. The very best way to relieve stress is a full immersion to nature without any distractions from material items. Plan a weekly family outing. The family can take a hike and collect pine cones, go camping, wild flower picking, fossil hunting, collecting bright colored fall leaves, berry picking, bird watching; anything to build a rewarding relationship with nature. Nature cures stress in children and adults.

Now if I may, I would like to end this workbook of children's numbers with a poem my father gave to me on my sixteenth birthday:

> I cannot ask you to smile all my smiles, cry all my tears,
> 	share all my hopes, dream all my dreams.
>
> For you have your own smiles, tears, hopes and dreams,
> 	which are yours alone.
>
> But if you wish to walk with me awhile,
> 	I will smile with your laughter, hurt in your tears,
> 		hope for your hopes and listen to your dreams.

> "The privilege of a lifetime is being who you are."
> 			- Joseph Campbell

CPSIA information can be obtained
at www.ICGtesting.com
Printed in the USA
BVHW092135230120
570324BV00005B/245